Look at the letters and say the sounds. See how quickly you can say all of them.

Say the sounds and blend them together to read the words. Where is the pin in the picture?

spin

Say the word *ants* and listen out for the sounds: *ants* – /a-n-t-s/. (There is one sound dot underneath the ants for each sound in the word.)

sit   pat